KIEV

RAZIM
LAKE

CRIMEA

BUCHAREST

LAKE
ATANASOVSKO
BURGAS

SVILENGRAD

EVROS
DELTA

BLACK
SEA

THE
BOSPHORUS

SYRIA

IRAN

N
W E
S

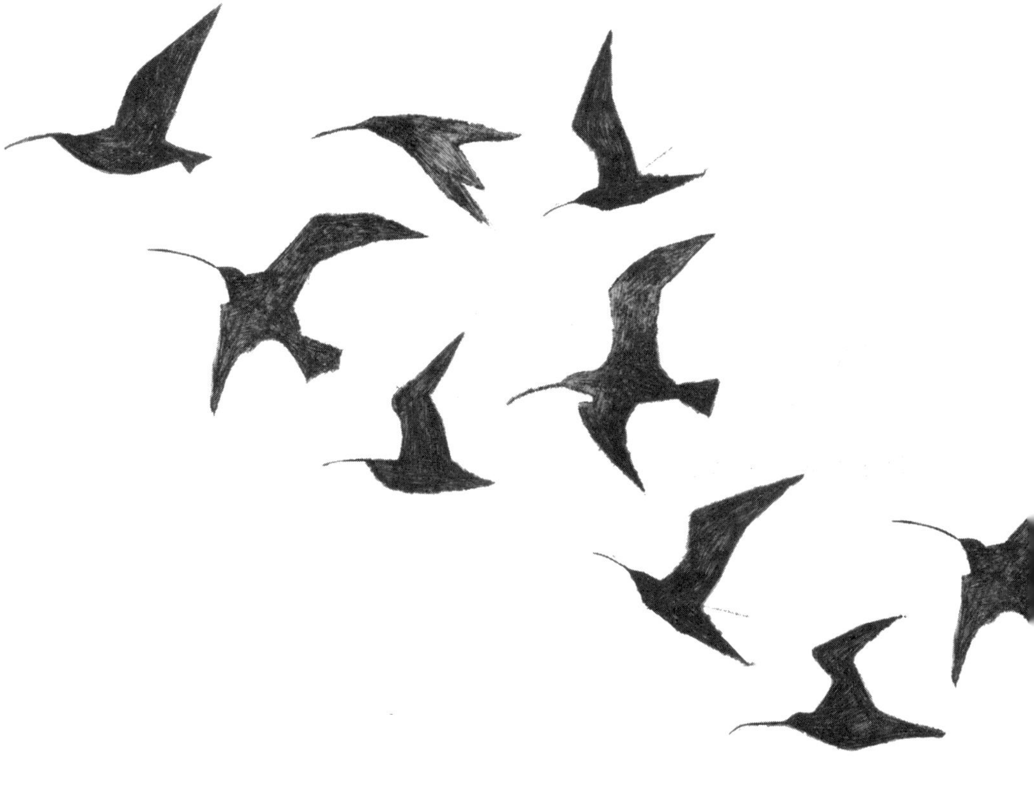

TO THE MEMORY OF MICHAEL JACOBS,
HIS WORK AND LIFE AND LOVE.

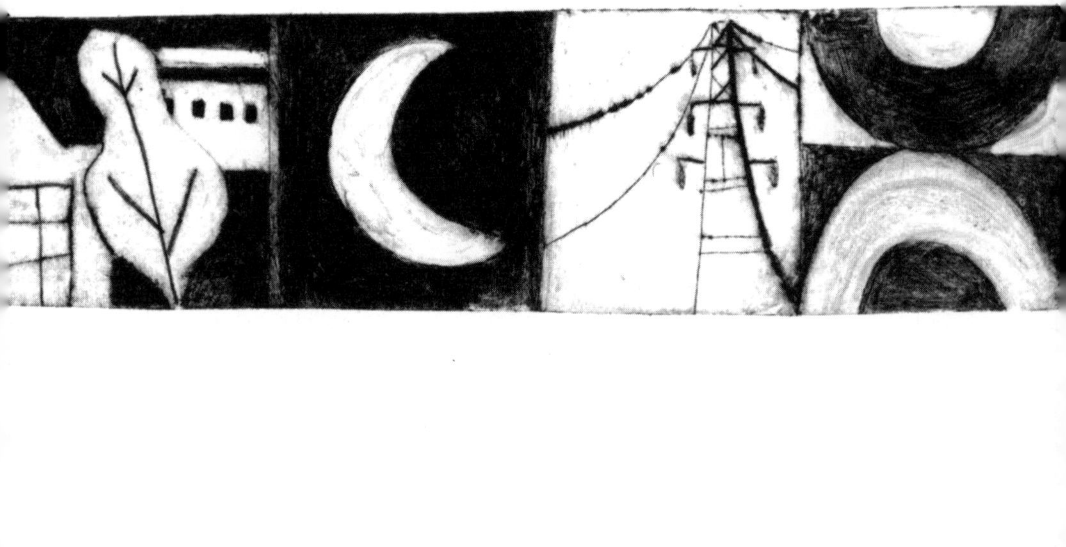

Orison for a Curlew

Horatio Clare

Illustrated by Beatrice Forshall

LITTLE TOLLER

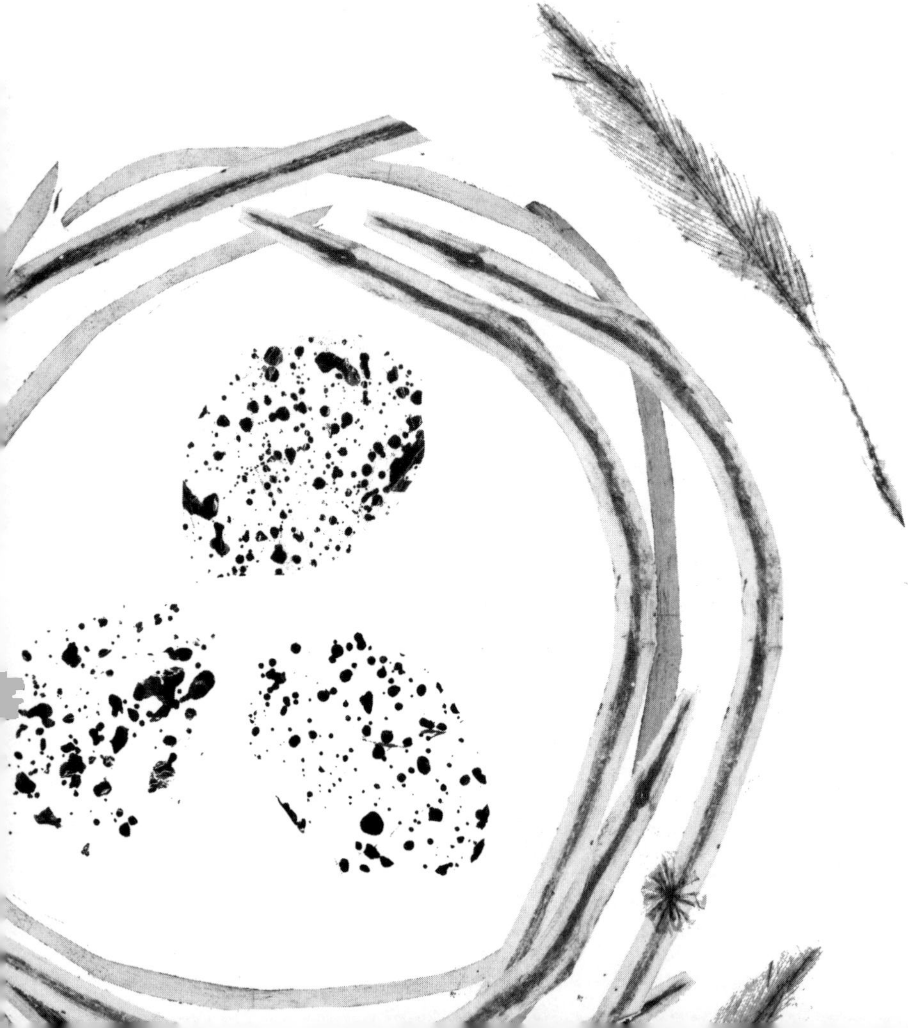

Contents

Introduction to a Ghost   9
The (Only) Government Ornithologist   17
A Ringtone on the Axios   25
East to Evros   33
By Accident to Bulgaria   43
Myth-busting in Transylvania   49
According to Mr Ushakov   61
The Hero of the Danube Delta   67
Bursts of Hope in Bulgaria   77
Lesson from a Ghost   91
Acknowledgements   99

Introduction
to a Ghost

When I was commissioned to tell the story of the western world's rarest bird it did, at least officially, still exist. It was a grail of the birding world. From the winter of 2009 to the spring of 2011 a huge international search saw teams of ornithologists scouring likely areas of eastern and southern Europe, North Africa and the Middle East – to the extent that vast swamps and impenetrable wetlands can be scoured.

From Serbia to Saudi Arabia, from Kazakhstan to the Maghreb, men and women went to the likeliest places (saltmarshes, lagoons, estuaries and deltas) at the most promising times (winter in the south and east, spring and autumn in Europe), levelled their binoculars, scanned with their telescopes, solicited local knowledge and advice, watched, waited, trudged, waded and hoped to see a beautiful creature, a species of curlew plumaged in a blend of whites and golds, with dark spots on the flanks, slim and graceful of form, more refined than the plumpy common curlew, with a thinner down-curving beak which makes it look as though it is chewing a stem of grass.

Very few people alive have seen a Slender-billed curlew, and for all their work and watching, none of the searchers was able to claim a definite sighting. There were some possible encounters, including a group of five glimpsed in the Crimea, but what was termed 'the final push' to find the Slender-billed curlew, *Numenius tenuirostris*, came to nothing.

The species is still listed as 'critically endangered' by the International Union for Conservation of Nature, but it is an open secret that the authorities of the bird world believe it is either extinct or as good as gone.

This year, existence having intervened with me (we had a baby, I wrote a book, we migrated from Italy to Britain) even while extinction may have been closing with the curlew, I set out to follow the trail of the bird, to tell its story, and to discover what happened to it. I knew I stood no chance of finding *Numenius tenuirostris* ('of slim beak and the new moon') even before consensus among conservationists removed it from the unofficial lists of the living. The last officially-accepted sighting was in Hungary in 2001, and this is contentious. The Hungarian Institute for Ornithology believes it, but similar organisations in other countries do not. You have to go back to 1999 to find verified records from Greece and Oman, though there have been various unconfirmed encounters since, including one in Oman this spring. Thus my grant from the Royal Geographical Society was given to fund an account of its passing, a tale that seems to begin with a mournful ending, though nothing about this story is as it first appears. While an account of the end of a species might seem destined to be gloomy, the human story that attends it is one of entirely counter-intuitive and quite marvellous success.

"The Slender-billed curlew has three problems," says George Handrinos, the father of modern Greek ornithology. "It is very rare, so to see one is a miracle. It is very difficult to identify, and it is very, very shy."

Handrinos uses the present tense deliberately. Proving negatives in this case being only marginally more difficult than asserting positives, the bird is now a kind of

Shrodinger's curlew, both alive and not.

Initially I saw my task as the compilation of a requiem for the opposite of the passenger pigeon: a creature largely unseen, scarcely considered, and hardly missed. As well as its marketing problem – it might with equal accuracy have been called the Golden curlew, about which we might have cared more – this bird seems to have formed a series of inadvertantly perilous habits.

Almost no terra incognita remains on what is becoming Terra Hominis, the planet of Man (a dozen species are estimated to collapse daily) but not even having had the wit to find a piece of wilderness seems to have helped our hero. Nesting behind the former Iron Curtain, near Tara in western Siberia, in a swathe of taiga swamps and marshes about twice the size of France should have been a good move. Nesting only there now looks like a slip.

Migrating over the Curtain via the Black Sea coast of the Balkans through Greece, southern Italy and the gun-happy islands of the Mediterranean to wintering grounds on North African coast was asking for it. The bird's favoured deltas, the Danube in Romania and the Evros in Greece, are thoroughly hunted. Italy jumps with shotgun-fire during migration season. Malta is a death-trap. When the flocks are on the move the shooting there goes on all day, then by torch and moonlight.

Surviving birds arrive on the coasts of Egypt and the Maghreb hungry, tired and flying low. Hundreds of miles of mist-nets await them. The unlucky are trapped and taken to bird markets, and if not sold for food, discarded.

Being a bird of the saltmarsh, of the littoral margins where earth, the great rivers, the sea and sky bleed into one another also placed the Slender-billed curlew in harm's way, as these regions have been drained, cultivated, desalinated, exploited and polluted.

And yet none of the specialists who think about the bird believes that hunting along its route or environmental degradation are responsible for its decline. Plenty of suitable habitat remains. The species was no more of a target for hunters than any other.

If it has gone it is the first avian extinction in the Western Palearctic since 1852 when the last Great Auk – a flightless, oceanic fowl – went the way of the dodo, eaten out of existence by sailors. The end of the auk was a sign that the oceans were now utterly within man's grasp. Plunder, pollution and over-fishing were about to surpass even the depredations of the whalers. The Slender-billed curlew might well have some similar message or signal for us – but what? And where to start looking for it?

Not so long ago your best chance of seeing *Numenius tenuirostris* was to travel to the Merja Zerga lagoons near Kenitra on Morocco's Atlantic coast. A small population wintered here and a pair were filmed in 1994: you can watch them online, vigourously alive, pecking, probing, feeding and regarding the camera with apparent insouciance. Until 1995 birdwatchers who wished to study it, or merely to tick the species off their to-see lists, made a hopeful pilgrimage here. I did, too. It was pointless. Yes, the lagoons have been somewhat drained, grazed and hunted, but they are still vigorous with avian life, including many of our target's common cousins. "Yes, I remember this bird," said a fisherman at the site. "It doesn't come here anymore. I don't know why."

Matching locations of observations with their times of year gives a calendar of previous appearances. I followed it to Sicily, to Italy and to the Evrotas delta in the Peloponnese, simultaneously hopeful and hopeless. No bird did I find, and no witness either, though there was a moment of wild hope in Evrotas, as a juvenile whimbrel flew straight towards my binoculars. They look very like Slender-billed curlews, but they are not.

"Any sign of your bird?" people began to ask, grinning. This year I changed approach. Instead of chasing a fowl that had disappeared I resolved to track down people who had not: the eye-witnesses and searchers along its route. At once a futile-seeming quest became a journey through time, societies and the Europe of living memory. Whatever else it has done, the Slender-billed curlew creates a link between generations, between eras, between cultures and between different stages in our relationship with the environment. This story begins in the cradle and, perhaps, the cenotaph of Euro-genic civilisation, Athens.

The (Only) Government Ornithologist

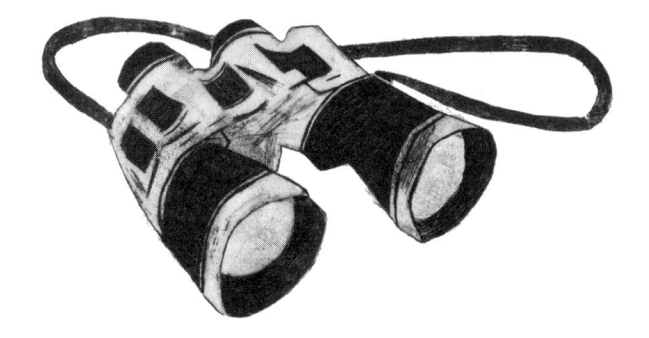

The bus route from the airport to Glyfada, a once fashionable seaside suburb of Athens, is lined with the detritus of a leisured society that no longer exists. Showrooms for swimming pools, boats, marble bathrooms and cars heap up, one after the other, in a slew of special offers, sales and tattering flags. Grand hotels in Glyfada have been replaced with tour-package blocks, basic places frequented by retirees from countries to the north who are on better pensions than their Greek equivalents.

Here I met George Handrinos, a man with a Zeus-like profusion of white mane and beard. He lives a few blocks from the front in a flat he says is more library than living space, with his wife and two unemployed sons. Maria, their mother, is suffering from a depression brought on by retirement from teaching English and sharpened by what Greeks refer to as 'the crisis'.

"I hate Greece and I hate the Greeks," she says, "I love England, Scotland, every single stone. I want to go to England and die there."

George remonstrates with her gently. He has the most beguiling smile; all his features squeeze and crease into a wizened and owlish beam. Recounting his Slender-billed curlew story makes him smile a lot, at first.

"My father was one of these old-fashioned hunters. He was in the country police so he was very strict about the laws, very disciplined. He shot birds of course. I remember holding a dead turtle dove, I was trying to draw the bird, the colours – I knew nothing about taxidermy but I was wondering how can I preserve this bird?"

In mid September 1972 George was helping out at his cousin's veterinary practice south of Thessaloniki. Also employed there was a young German.

"I was talking to this man outside the building and suddenly an eagle! An eagle passing above and quite low, a big white bird with black spots. I had no idea what it was, it was soaring. He rushed inside, got binoculars, came out and I said 'What are you doing?' 'Birdwatching!' he said, 'It's a big hobby in Germany!' Nobody had told me – it was really a revelation – you can study birds without shooting them. He showed me Petersen's field guide. I went to the big international bookshop but they didn't have it. They had the Collins, it was new. I bought a copy. I borrowed binoculars. Went back. It was a short-toed eagle. Fantastic!

"At that time we had a dictatorship so to go out with binoculars was to risk being arrested as a pervert or something. But not far from the village is a delta of three rivers, small lagoons and a big area of mud flats and saltmarshes and reed beds. I sat with the guide on my lap. Within one day I counted one hundred and fifteen species. That was amazing."

His face lights up again.

"I remember I learned all the Latin names in a month! Not the Greek. In that period we didn't have Greek names for all the species. Then I met another fellow, we became friends, we had no car, nothing, at that time, so we used to watch birds in Athens, swallows and robins. After four years we joined the Hellenic Society for Nature Protection and formed a small group of birdwatchers."

Handrinos became the only ornithologist employed by the Greek government, head of the Hellenic Ornithological

Society and the go-to man in Greece for international organisations concerned for the welfare of birds. When he dies, he says, he would like to be remembered for his work on establishing the Dadia reserve in the forests of Thrace, and his efforts at protecting the wildfowl of the Evros delta in the same far eastern region of Greece. The river Evros forms the border with Turkey. Debouching into the sea it creates a 20,000 hectare wetland of vital ecological significance, one of the last known haunts of the Slender-billed curlew in Europe.

"My first obsevation of the species was the 16th of January 1986 during the winter waterfowl count when we saw four birds at Evros," Handrinos says. "The second observation was the 4th of April 1988 also at Evros. We saw two and we were very confident they were Slender-billed curlews.

"The first time I remember well. It was a very sunny but very cold day. We had just started doing the counts in the north, counting ducks in the lagoon. We saw a flock of common curlews. They landed close to four other birds. We realised these were smaller, much smaller, and we were very lucky to compare the two species. When you see them together you can tell. They were feeding together in the water. As soon as we put the telescope on them they flew away.

"The first reaction when you see such a bird – it's like seeing, what? A dinosaur? You know this is a species on the brink of extinction. You are very excited of course but you have a bitter feeling that this is a species that is going to die – I am looking at a relic, at a fossil, it's a kind of strange feeling really. Bitter-sweet.

"What can I do for these birds? To share the knowledge that's one thing. To save the habitat that's one thing. To stop the hunting that's another. But you know deep inside it's very difficult. It's not an easy thing to do."

The 2009–11 search organised by BirdLife International, the Royal Society for the Protection of Birds in Britain and sister organisations across Europe was a remarkable effort. Backing up the searchers were groups of expert bird ringers, prepared to fly to the site of a confirmed observation in the hope of capturing a bird and tagging it with a satellite tracker. If only something – anything – could be learned about the movements of the species it might be possible, so the thinking went, to protect areas of breeding, passage and wintering.

In Greece, George Handrinos first collected all the records of the species in that country since the late nineteenth century. With little funding available and cuts falling on every department of the Greek government no great effort was affordable.

"We made this chart and distributed it to many birdwatchers. We still keep our eyes open for them but we have had not even a possible sighting. Last year we had one record from not far from Thessaloniki but it turned out to be a normal curlew. The last record in Greece was in 1999 in the Evrotas delta."

In his retirement Handrinos has found a new passion: trains. He is particularly interested in the Second World War, during which large parts of the Greek railway system were destroyed. It is a period which has recently become fashionable with many Greek students and researchers. Greeks claim theirs was the only country not compensated after the conflict. Should Germany make good on its debt now, they say, it would wipe out the country's deficit. Without faith in their politicians, a compensation miracle seems as likely as effective economic reform.

"When I started my career I believed that if you gave politicians good scientific data things would change. One of my disadvantages was to believe for many years that good scientific data was everything. No it's not. Not for politicians it's not. I begged the ministry, please, just two or three signs near Alexandroupolis airport. Five miles to your left is Evros, a wetland reserve of international importance! Nothing. No signs, nowhere, nowhere. Look, in Greece we have sun, landscape, history and environment. If you don't look after the environment, what do you have to sell?"

Our interview finishes with lunch in a near-deserted taverna on the seafront. An uncle of one of Maria's former pupils approaches our table, selling lottery tickets. Money, Handrinos says, is not the whole story.

"You don't always need money for conservation. Two or three lorries for ten days would clean all the rubbish out of the Evros delta. Governments use money as an excuse. They just don't want to do it."

A Ringtone on the Axios

The night train from Athens to Thessaloniki is a wonderfully cheap and communal form of transport. My compartment contained Sudoku-addicted sisters-in-law, one of whom had the bearing of a nun, her husband, who had the smile, sweat and contours of a gourmand, and a young man on his way to join the police force. We slept, more or less, intertwined.

Thessaloniki was a beautiful city in the 1980s, before it was overrun by cars, according to Yannis Tsougrakis. He is one of the successors of the pioneer generation of Handrinos, former head of the Hellenic Ornithological Society for northern Greece. He foresaw the closure of his office, however, and changed jobs, becoming a civil servant attached to the university of Thessaloniki where he works in the sustainability office. A staff of seven has been cut to two, sustainability not being fashionable these days, he says.

Vigorous and dry, married to a kindergarten teacher and the father of an eight year-old son, Yannis Tsougrakis is avowedly rational in his approaches.

"I am not the kind of birdwatcher-twitcher. I am a conservationist. The starting point is conservation. For most birdwatchers in Greece of my generation you can say that. The new generation are not interested in conservation as we were: now they are interested in taking many photographs – it's like a sport.

"Last year there was a risk I would lose my job but I

didn't. It was a matter of luck. I feel safe, more or less. Safety comes from comparison with others. My wife and I still have our jobs. But we are living on the edge. We are using our reserves. The feeling of safety is – if something bad happens to us thousands more will be dying. There will be people dying on the streets, which is not far from being true. People are abandoning children and babies, which happened in the thirties and forties."

My grant, the Neville Shulman Challenge Award, "aims to further the understanding and exploration of the planet: its cultures, peoples and environments." As Yannis talks I feel that the stories of the lives of men like him and Handrinos, who personify the creation and nuturing of ornithology and conservation in Greece, are just as important as the story of the bird, which links them.

We thread our way through Thessaloniki's traffic and turn south-west towards the sea, where two deltas, the Axios and Aliakmonas, and the estuaries of Gallikos and Loudias rivers combine. Olympus overlooks us through a distant hill haze. We pass tamarisk and bull rush, little memorial shrine chapels by the road, and the smell of the marshes fills the air, tang and tart, then gaseous and methane; brackish bitten smells, and sweet succulent smells of samphire and salt herbs. The size of the marshes, lagoons, the river systems and the delta proper beyond them, a mosaic of green and pinking salicornia glasswort beds, entirely inaccessible except by punt or boat, make any search hopeless, any hope of systematic coverage futile, ridiculous.

"The Slender-billed curlew has always been legendary," Yannis says.

"I claim to have seen it twice in my life, both times in bad observation conditions. Once in Evros in 1999. A male hen harrier went over flying low, and he flushed a curlew – I saw it flying for 1.5 seconds – which was clearly different, smaller and paler. At the same spot the next day there was a definite observation, so this was one.

"And another one at Axios, again it was a very different curlew at the roost – far away against the sun with a telescope – but in the same spot my friend Savas saw one, one or two days before. What does it feel like? In these cases disappointment! You cannot say 'Yes!' You cannot be one hundred percent sure. Yes, definitely, dissapointment. You cannot be sure so you cannot be satisfied."

"So what do you think happened to it?" I ask.

"I don't think I have an answer that relies on facts. We don't have any facts. Our lack of knowledge is almost complete about this bird. We couldn't do anything other than go searching for it. When we were searching I always had the feeling the bird was behind our backs laughing at us. We were looking at the wet, at the lagoon – it was behind us in the dry grassland. We spent lots of hours and days studying and discussing and organising. I don't know if it has ever been numerous. You question your own observations, then you question others. You acccept hard proofs only. In the past someone's word, or my word, nobody would question it. Now you question yourself. Was it really?"

"And if it has gone," I want to know, "does it matter?"

He pauses and puffs out his cheeks, speaks slowly at first, then becomes increasingly excited.

"For me the extinction of a species is something very big. It doesn't have to link with something. It's like a taboo – something extremely big by itself. We don't know what happened to it – was it human driven or not? You can have symposia, eat, discuss, drink, have orgies! Anyone can have his opinion! The failure of an ecosystem may be initially driven by man but that affects other species – the butterfly effect. Without the knowledge there is no value in it; if you cannot find the reason. We are in a time when everything starts from man but we usually categorise things in terms of how we have to deal with them. It is very difficult to deal with this in terms of conservation measures. Conservation is about action, to do something, or to reverse something. Not just to know – to act! If I can't act it's just documentary; just information."

As we drive along the seaward road, to the east of the Gallikos, the Axios a distant line of trees, the birds are first to the landward side: redshank, knot, ducks, gulls, pygmy cormorants, stilts and flamingoes.

Then the coast turns west and the rock breakwater runs along a richer, sloping dyke, with footprints of vegetation and islets in the sea. Now there are curlew every hundred meters, like sentries evenly spaced, a line of watchers. There are greenshank on the mudbanks and martins in the air. A snake crosses the road. We pass lines of fishermen's houses leaning into the wind. Large and ominous black dogs keep watch and stalk the landward strands. An observation tower has replaced one that burned, a sturdy thing with nets and flags flinging and flapping in the wind. We reach a point within range of the Axios where the curlews roost and the track turns south across the delta to sandbars in the middle distance. It runs down to a dip and submerges.

"We could go through but it's salt and I would have to wash the car," Yannis says. (I think it's pride in his Fiat 'goat', as he calls it, that raises the possibility: there is a lot more water ahead.) So we dismount, and put up the telescope, and enter the delta evening.

There is a lighthouse due south, to the right of it a low island with a pale structure.

"That was Aphrodite's taverna. They were an old couple, and she was called Aphrodite. It was perfect, however hot it was – and in July it is really impossible – there was always wind there and never any mosquitos. You could get there on a boardwalk. We would go and stay until dusk or all night if it was a full moon. The only thing was because they fried everything in the same oil, everything – the fish, the calamaris, cuttlefish – they all tasted the same!"

We study curlews through the scope; it is a perfect time for them, they are grouping, feeding. The English collective noun is a herd of curlews, an unusual and dissonant term for a bird. But the common curlew is a plump-looking creature, beautifully speckled in tawny plumage, with its long decurving beak. They look warm even when they are up to their thighs in cold water, as they often are. When large numbers take flight together they fill the sky with a tumbled untidy jumbling of cries and white rumps and strident flapping; 'herd' describes them well. Their music is the sound of all their habitats, of the marsh, the moor and the sky, a hectic and melodious trilling which gave them their English name. In French it is even better – *courlis*: courlee! In Greek it is *tourlida*: toourleeeda!

Yannis recalls hearing a cry like it, but unlike it: the call of the Slender-billed mystery.

"It was like a shock. I was out birdwatching three years ago, in early September. I was here, close to this roost of curlews. I have a Slender-billed curlew ringtone. I heard exactly the same noise. I hear it every day, I hear it every time I get a text message, it is imprinted in my brain – I heard it and I thought I received a message. And then I realised it was not a message. The phone was in the car. I went back for days but nothing."

He agrees to play the Slender-billed curlew's cry from his phone. It takes him a while to find it but then he does. It rises and rises, a burbling ache, a fluted whistle with lament and wildness and defiance in it, a sound for the whole evening, for time gone, for taboos crushed, for mystery, for Greece.

East to Evros

The little port of Alexandroupolis is the last coastal town before the Turkish border, most of a day's train ride from Thessaloniki into the hills of Thrace. Leaving Thessaloniki you pass miles of abandoned trains: rolling stock, engines and carriages eaten by rust and vegetation. It is an awful, eerie sight – ten miles of them drawn up in parallels, so twenty, thirty miles of carriages, immovable, the oldest submerging, the future's archaeology.

Olympus has a flat conical crest atop its wide ridge summits, a mountain on a mountain, perfect for the Gods. As our early train curves north and east they are breakfasting up there, Zeus lazily chucking olives into his maw; Aphrodite slow and drowsy from her short sleep, bed-headed; Hephaestus drinking coffee – he's been up since the dark, has something cooking on the forge – Athene eating muesli, checking her iPad: she'd like to retire but her projects are never done, because we will not learn wisdom. Artemis appears with a pair of turtle doves. She wants to roast them with almonds. George Handrinos and Yannis Tsougrakis both say hunting is down, marginally, because of the crisis. Most of the hunting clubs are called Artemis, Yannis said. "They are very powerful," George said, darkly. "It's all dirty politics with them."

Now the land becomes dreamy, sunflowers hanging burned heads like choirs of the penitent dead, shepherds with small flocks in a punishing heat which swells outside.

A mother slaps her daughter, a blow you could hear the length of the carriage, but does not make the little girl cry. She retreats; a few minutes later they are getting on wonderfully and the mother deals a mock-blow to the same place which turns into a stroke, part in penitence, part in chiding. The heat grows and grows until the shadows hide under the bushes. Poplars and birches give way to acacia and thorn. In the early afternoon we came down to the sea, and the port of Alexandroupolis, which gazes across the Aegean to the island of Samothraki.

When Philip II of Macedon sailed from Samothraki with his new wife Olympias (Plutarch says they were betrothed at once) and they looked towards the shore, they saw this skyline. The foothills of the Rhodope mountains rise to the north and west in pined swells; to the east they fall in descending curves down to the Enos hills on the banks of the great river Evros, which now separates Greece from Turkey. Philip would have marked its outflow, a wide wild green delta, tangled then with high trees and thick vegetation to landward, flattening into a 20,000 hectare mosaic of marsh grasses and samphire pools, reeds and plashings, lagoons and sinuous channels. Even from a mile or two offshore he would have seen clouds of birds. Some are very big, the white Dalmatian pelicans, the black storks and the flamingoes, others too small to be seen from much distance, and one, we believe, would have been shy even then, in 357 BC.

It is quite possible that Olympias and Philip did see Slender-billed curlews, though, because our bird used to congregate in large flocks, perhaps huge flocks. During the second half of the nineteenth century, the experts say, its populations were more dense than those of its common cousin. In the story of its decline, its crash out of the world, which begins in the 1920s, there are extraordinary flashes of a younger planet. In October 1978, 150 were seen here, in the Evros marshes. In the same place in 1983, 250 were reported. Philip and Olympias may well have seen 1,000 in a gold-white straggle along the shore.

The frustrations of George Handrinos over the signposting of the Evros delta, a few kilometres east of Alexandroupolis, are still justified. There is almost nothing to indicate the existence of one of the most important reserves in southern Europe, and the bus driver, who passes the Evros Delta Conservation Centre every day, had never noticed it. One of his passengers had, fortunately. Here I meet Vasilis Elias, a young man with the easy lope of a ranger. Vasilis is a warden at Evros; its lagoons and dykes are his workplace.

Until two years ago the delta was a way into Europe for refugees from the Middle East and Africa. Since the erection of a fence along the border clandestine immigration has here fallen away.
    "The main problem now is illegal hunting and fishing," Vasilis says. "The hunting is mostly for geese and ducks, and mostly for sport. The hunters are Greeks and Cypriots, they come from Athens, the Peloponnese, Crete. If we catch them hunting illegal species they get a fine. They are allowed a three-shot shotgun: many have five, six, seven shot guns. Every year the Forestry Service publishes guidelines of what is allowed; you are allowed 12 mallard, but no shelduck. Also we often find people hunting at night – it is illegal after sunset.
    "I go into the delta every day, often with visitors. Until three or four years ago we had 10,000 visitors a year; now it is 3,000 a year. Most come from all over Greece; about 20 percent are foreign, mostly central Europe, also Britain, the

Netherlands, Germany. Foreigners mostly come in spring, Greek tourists in summer. Many are from universities, student groups studying, and I often go with special groups of birdwatchers.

"Our main goals are protecting, managing and promoting the delta. The biggest problem in Evros is fresh water. Many drainage canals were made 50 years ago. They dug a network of channels: the Evros used to meander, it was made straight to dry the area and cultivate the land. As a result half the area is cultivated and half protected. The delta is 20,000 hectares, half protected. We can't do big works, we can't reverse what has been done. We do small things – stopping new extractions, protecting water and birds."

Vasilis helps me take my bearings. From the north the Loutros river runs into the delta, it is dry in summer. The Evros rises on the Rila mountain near Sofia and splits in two under the Enos hills on the Turkish border. The eastern delta is a military zone. The hills to the north are the Rhodope mountains which run into Macedonia. The railway is the delta's northern border, at west the airport, at east the mountains, at south the Thracian sea. Approached from the centre, the delta's northern peripheral zone is cultivated with cotton and wheat, and bees in blue hives. The island of Samothraki floats on the horizon, a mountain ship with a cargo of cloud.

We survey Drana lagoon, centre of Slender-billed curlew sightings for all of Greece. It is a wide and islanded expanse, with strands of sand, flamingoes, pelicans, a marsh harrier, the smell of salt sea and samphire. The wind is strong from the north, force five, the weather clear, the sun hot. Saltmarsh with glasswort makes perfect curlew country:

the birds keep their familiar sentry spacings, a regular force, not as numerous as they were in the Axios until we reach the coast. We visit all the accessible Slender-billed curlew sighting spots: they were almost all seen from the tracks. The saltwater Drana lagoon was used for fish farming until 1987, then drained by the locals who believed the salt was destroying surrounding cultivated land. They blocked the only channel to the sea, opened a dyke and pumped the water out. The following year they agreed to restore water to the lagoon, but fresh water. The restoration of saltwater in 2004 represents a real triumph, particularly from the point of view of the Slender-billed curlew, which has always favoured the seaward part of the delta, and was seen in areas where seaside alkali grasses and glassworts grow. Both need salt. We study every curlew we see through binoculars as a matter of course. They are lovely creatures but they are not our bird.

"Do you think you will know it if you see it?" Vasilis asks.

If it is close enough, yes, of course, I say. But otherwise no. I think of Handrinos and Tsougrakis and the brevity of their sightings. You could be sure of possiblity, and equally sure of uncertainty.

Vasilis aims his glasses at other birds.

"I like glossy ibises," he says, "I just like them! I don't like cormorants. We have to ring them, they are really difficult, offensive birds. Offensive dirty birds! I don't like gulls. They are all over Alexandroupolis, and they eat everything, they eat other birds' eggs."

We cross to the western side of the delta, the salt swamp. To get there we drive through kilometres of cultivated cotton.

"We had so much rain this year the cotton grew too high. And we ran out of pesticide – Greece ran out of pesticide.

We had to order it in from Italy."

Happily it does not seem to have entirely worked, as flies invade the car and outside a shrike passes while a flock of bee-eaters dive in the wind, fluting and turning, that wonderful flared-wing banking which catches the light in their splayed feathers. Suddenly they are flinging about, swallows too, as a sparrowhawk thrusts through the low air and everything jumps and turns around her.

Vasilis talks about the changes brought by the crisis.

"I used to travel three times a year, but now maybe once every two years. My father was a plumber. He told my brother, if you are a plumber you will never be rich but you will always have work. But now he doesn't. There was so much new building, now there is none. He works in a bar in the evenings in town. My girlfriend is a teacher – Greek. I would love to see northern Europe, I would love to see Sweden and Japan! But I am lucky I have a salary. It is reduced, but, living here, 20 minutes from the office is the beach. And I am in the delta every day."

This part of the delta, heading north-west to the sea, is a mosaic of secret pools, mysterious waters, deep overgrown channels, high marsh plants and reeds. A huge cloud of black storks jump up like an ambush of Hussars in their red bills and leggings, white fronts and dark uniforms. They look like chinstrap guardsmen with scarlet swords. They are on migration: these will go down the coast, cross the Bosphorus and the Sinai and bear south to Africa. The black stork has been known to kill one of its young in times of scarcity, the weakest, to ensure the survival of the rest. A spartan of a bird then, ruthless and martial, a fighter. This is another Slender-billed curlew area, wind-blown, light-flung, gull-cried, the sea's green edge. Reeds rattle, shifting the horizon of these level-changing littorals of water, earth and sky. The delta is a co-operation between the sea and the river, the flotsam and accumulations of both comprise it. The sea's trophies and the river's burdens heap and mulch to make this rune-riddled spreading.

"What does the Slender-billed curlew mean to you, Vasilis? Does it mean anything, in fact?"

"When I started to work here I first came across the Slender-billed curlew in reports and documents, the rarest bird in Europe that had been seen in the delta. Many old restrictions that are still in force are based on the Slender-billed curlew. And other species, but the Slender-billed curlew was very important. Even now the hunters say why don't you allow hunting there? Because of the Slender-billed curlew? No one has seen it! It doesn't exist! 10,000 protected hectares and the hunters don't recognise the studies, they say it was never here, or it hasn't been seen for many decades."

I feel like cheering: here, suddenly, is another part of the puzzle, another part of the story! All at once the bird's legacy is more than a collectable Moroccan postage stamp: it was fundamental to the protection of the delta. All these glittering prizes of water and light, the birds, the plants, the insects and the scents, these are partly its gift.

"And suppose we saw one, would it make a difference?"

"If we saw one now, it would maybe change the laws. It would change where you could go with vehicles, when and where you could hunt. Many people would come to search for it. I would be monitoring it. Visitors still come and ask for it now. Last year a visitor asked for it – they ask if you've seen it, where it was. Here it's already a myth, a legend. Many of us have heard of it but nobody has seen it. For all lost species the human factor is the greatest – pollution, presence, pesticides, water, cultivation, drainage, even noise."

We reach the sea, where our bird has been seen on the strand. "I think you need to wait, and watch, and observe," Vasilis says, but we both know it would take a hermit's time and patience, and, he believes, bring nothing. Just where a sighting was made is another curlew, and beyond are a scattered herd of them. They jump and blow away with the wind.

By Accident
to Bulgaria

Some notes on twenty-first century train travel in Greece and the Balkans, first. In Greece it is common for the departure boards to be broken or blank: information about which trains are expected on which platforms is communicated orally by station staff. Station staff are indistinguishable from passengers, though some carry walkie-talkies. In Bulgaria it is common for no departure board to exist and for platforms to be unnumbered. Determining the names of stations from the train can also be difficult. In Romania the situation is better; station staff wear magnificent red caps, stations are named and platforms numbered.

My intention was to travel back to Thessaloniki and take the daily train to Sofia, there to catch the train to Bucharest. In Bucharest I was due to meet an ornithologist and Slender-billed curlew seeker, Istavan Moldovan, and travel with him to the Danube delta south of Tulcea. From Tulcea I planned to take buses down the Black Sea coast to Chenge Skele, near Burgas in Bulgaria, a noted migration point and Slender-billed curlew sighting spot.

All these plans went awry, in process if not in upshot, when I boarded the wrong train out of Alexandroupolis. Instead of heading west to Thessaloniki this train went north to the Bulgarian border, following the Evros valley parallel to the Turkish frontier. Irrigation, agriculture and the conversion of what would have once been flood plain to farmed land is clear as the train follows the river. Channels, pumps and drainage ditches are everywhere apparent. Even after a summer of exceptionally high rainfall in the area the river lay low between dry banks. If curlews did once find sustenance in the Evros valley it is clear that it would be much harder now: the land is dry, and no *Numenius* species were observed.

Crossing the border into Bulgaria at Svilengrad I took a bus, then a train north-west, first to Dimitrovgrad in eastern Bulgaria, then to Plovdiv. At Plovdiv I caught a train to Sofia.

To a traveller accustomed to the dense populations of western Europe Bulgaria is a shock. The population has been shrinking for the last 20 years: two million Bulgarians, predominantly those of prime working age, live abroad. Birth rates are among the lowest in the world while death rates are among the highest. You travel through a semi-abandoned country. The signature sight of the countryside is the collapsing house. On the edge of every town and village formerly excellent dwellings, Italianate in style, red-tiled and extensive, are falling down and derelict. Everywhere you look roofs are caving in. Every town of any size is surrounded by disintegrating factories and industrial units. The effect on the spirits of the inhabitants can easily be imagined: "This is Bulgaria," said Roman Tsolovoa, a student I met when our train broke down outside Dimitrovgrad. "Many links are missing."

Bulgaria is the most corrupt country in the European Union. One billion euros in payments from Brussels were blocked last year because the money was going astray. In the south-east of the country an EU-funded new motorway has apparently died of starvation: huge amounts of money have been spent on its construction but it lies unfinished.

Young Roman, 22, plans to stay in Bulgaria; he is patriotic

and has a deep care for his country, his family and that of his girlfriend, Dianna. He says he can barely sleep for thinking of ways to help them all. He is studying biology in Plovdiv, commuting three times a week from Dimitrovgrad where his parents live. We meet when the train – a smart, new, EU-funded vehicle – breaks down in a tiny station, Stalevo, which sits, by the smell of the night and the sound of the cicadas, amid wide grassland and pasture. Roman is limping badly: he had to kick one of his father's dogs when it went for him.

His story seems illustrative of Bulgaria's current situation. Roman's girlfriend, Dianna, works at Sunny Beach, a resort on the Burgas coast notorious for bacchanalia. "There are drunk bodies sleeping in the streets and they are all English!" Roman laughs. Dianna's parents are both in London, her father is in construction, her mother is a cleaner. Roman's sister is a finance graduate who is waitressing in America. Roman's free time is given to planning and experimenting with business ideas. "I want success most," he says, "not money. Money is a bonus."

His ideas include sweet potatoes, which are not common in Bulgaria, and the propagation of a particular species of fast-growing tree. He asks that I do not share its name.

"The sad thing," he says, "is the old people who gave their life to the country and now they have nothing. My grandmother worked for 30 years as a cook, cooking for miners. Now she has less than a 100 euro a month. Many old people are alone with very little money." At the same time, he says, Bulgaria's postion as a country of transit between east and west means there are many ways to make illegal money. "Mootras", a kind of thick-necked gangster, are a common species, he says.

★

Roman is waiting in Plovdiv to meet Dianna off her train from the coast. He will escort her back to Dimitrovgrad for a couple of days. He is, he agrees, a very good boyfriend. He normally uses his travel time to study – today was English vocabulary, so I am useful to him. We pass our wait in Plovdiv, from midnight to 5 a.m., talking, eating kebabs and dozing on benches in the station. The night trains are packed: "People travel at night because it is 3 or 4 lev cheaper and it is cooler – there is no air conditioning," Roman says. The saving is equivalent to just over one British pound.

The Sofia train is sprawled with legs, arms and unconscious faces, as if it brings casualties from the front. There is a powerful, warm smell of bodies, tired, creaturely, smoky and perfumed with a sweet and popular scent.

In Sofia a message comes from Istavan Moldovan in Romania that he cannot now do the journey to the coast: his business demands he go to Hungary for a couple of days. He has found a substitute for me, he says, a keen birdwatcher who will organise the trip, drive the car and show me the Slender-billed curlew areas south of the Danube delta, in return for his expenses. This man, Cristian Mihai, is a noted bird photographer and will relish the opportunity to practice his art. I accept the substitute gratefully, but am resolved to meet Istavan Moldovan. He seems, from the tenor of his emails, a remarkable man. He was part of the Slender-billed curlew search in Egypt. I feel he is crucial to the story and tell him so. He says he could meet me in Sighisoara, Transylvania. It is a 1,000 kilometres from Sofia to Sighisoara via Bucharest, and back to Bucharest, but I am resolved to interview Moldovan, and Sighisoara is a medieval jewel of a hill town in central Transylvania. I set off at once.

Myth-busting in Transylvania

Sofia in a pink dawn smells of trees and cats. Sofia Gare Centrale is being torn down. Very few of the flourescent tubes in the ceiling of the main concourse work, so a huge space is cast in an undersea gloom. Light comes from the bright little kiosks, giving the effect of an uncleaned fishtank wrapped with Christmas tree lights. Bulgaria is a great repository of western obsolescence. I have seen old British police vans and a retired England-Wales-Scotland locomotive, the 'George Eliot', enjoying a second life. Time drapes himself over our slow train, head propped on hand, as if he has never hurried.

The wheels click-beat the rails as we follow a river valley north past dozy dolomitic scenery in ageing lemon sunlight; old man's beard grows beside the track, still young. A running white goat is the only thing in a hurry I have yet seen in Bulgaria. When we pause at the bigger stations, mostly unnamed, men pass down the train tapping the wheels with hammers. Each wheel answers with a lovely 'ching!' which says we are safe to continue. We pass vast fields of purple sunflowers and plains like steppes, autumn's yellow fingers thickening as we go north. Now single combine harvesters appear in seas of sunflowers, valiantly shearing, like lone tanks reaping all the armies of antiquity. Cattle stand in a river and toss their heads. Now we sweep through green channels jewelled with fruit - apples, plums and damsons.

In the afternoon we cross the leaden Danube, the train

ginger on a great iron bridge, as though we are suspended by rusty nails and precedent. The first sights of Romania are dreadful: rotting concretre tenaments below which men pick through rubbish bins. A boy in a slovenly park makes throwing gestures at the train, his face contorted.

Much of the industrial infrastructure is still smashed and abandoned, but more houses are occupied. There is a denser population and more money evident, with trains half the age of Bulgaria's and electricty to spare for illuminated signs and CCTV.

After a changing in Bucharest and crossing a dauntingly wide plain, so vast even the sky seemed to shrink from it, night falls as the land begins to rise around us. Romania shows little light out here; rare villages with lamps glowing behind curtains, but otherwise there is only darkness and the smell of fields and woods. The moon is an occluded smoked orange behind cloud, the night warm and still. People switch off their compartment lights; we travel in darkness. At Sighisoara, at midnight, a fellow traveller in an act of extraordinary kindess that seems to bemuse him gives me a lift up to the old town. Marius described himself as 'a functionary, nothing interesting'. He had made the five hour journey from Bucharest to pick up his son, 16 and 'sick' – 'family problem' – and take him back on a train at 2 a.m. He did not have time to be searching the old town's streets for a tourist's hotel, but he insisted on doing it.

In the morning, at 9 a.m. precisely, after a breakfast which includes bear salami, Istavan 'Steve' Moldovan bounces through the guesthouse gate. He is a broad man in his prime, dark hair retreating and cut short, intense olive-coloured eyes and a double crease below his brows like the mark of a problem-solver. He laughs as I marvel at the beauty of Sighisoara, its medieval streets, towers and steep-tiled roofs; it seems ready for snow and sleigh bells.

"I thought you would like it," he says. "I live 60 kilometres away."

"You were up early!"

"Oh I cannot sleep more than six hours, I wish I could."

He does not have a wife or children, he says – "Birdwatching, my passion, takes all my time! There is only time for work and my hobby."

We sit at a cafe table; he orders breakfast, having chided the waitress, with great humour, for looking defeated as she listed the unavailable items on the menu. "Don't tell me what you haven't got, tell me what you have!"

Steve, as he prefers to be called, speaks swiftly.

"I am Romanian, Hungarian and German. My grandmother was German Saxon and my grandfather from the Szeckler people of Eastern Transylvania. I am selling bill acceptors for cash machines, slot machines. When I returned from Egypt I was working for a company that did it. I swore when I turned 40 I wouldn't work for anybody else, so I kept my promise, I quit, left them, and I am building up my own company – we open in one month.

"No family! It's not about business but about birding. I am intersted in data-deficient species, extra-limital species. The research take weeks, there is no money in it, but I am interested; I look at it and I do it!

"For example, Cetti's Warbler. It isn't in Romania – it wasn't. I looked at the Bulgarian database. The Danube is the border, but at one place it turns north, the southern shore was in Romania. I had seen the bird in Turkey, I knew its habitats – people were always looking in reeds but it doesn't just like reeds – so I found the right habitat, went there at the right time, played the call. For three days I played the call, nothing. On the fourth day I was sitting having a cigarette and I heard it. I thought it was the call I had been playing in my head! But I found it. In a few days there were 20 birders there. But it took one year of research and four days of searching.

"Most of us are amateur birders. In 2007–8 it became a job, there was EU funding, people got involved and there was a salary. You'll never find a Romanian name in naturalism in the eighteenth and nineteenth century, Germans, French . . . My parents were naturalists and trekkers. My father was a lepidopterist; I was interested – no one else from my generation was. I was in high school, I was 16, I had a book, the 1983 edition of Guy Mountfort's *Birds of Europe*. It was winter and I was sitting at home watching the birds my mother fed, lots of birds, tits on the windowsill. I took the book and several days and started identifying species, looking at the distribution maps.

"In 1991 we were nine guys and a piece of paper: we called ourselves the Birding Society of Timuresc, the Milvus group, Latin for Red kite. We linked up with the Romanian Ornithological Society and became the Timuresc branch. The president and director had money from the RSPB, and binoculars and telescopes, and there are one or two more years of funding, but after that they will have to survive somehow.

"I was born in 1974, the Communist era, under Ceausescu. Every name was Romanised, so though I am ethnic Hungarian my name sounds Romanian. I was in the security force. I was a sportsman, fencing for 12 years and judo. I was supported by the army and state for one year and six months. It was a steady job with good money. What did we do? Nothing. Nothing! If the commander said what are you doing? Oh, cleaning this car! The second he has gone you stopped. It was a comedy, a parody. And then we joined the NATO forces and I had to go with soldiers, behave like an asshole, and one day I said I'm out.

"Under Communism nobody was sitting in the street and smoking, everyone had something to do, even if it was picking up garbage or foresting. No mobiles, no stress, burden free. OK you couldn't listen to the BBC or whatever, and long hair was a big deal at that time. I wore mine long because it wasn't allowed. My mother was in administration at a sugar factory, a neighbour was in a meat factory, you bartered.

"I went to study biology at university, I was interested in taxonomy, but already I was disappointed. I wished to work in birding and biology but no one's interested in conservation. They're interested in their jobs. They write and give the reports that they are asked for, no one really cares. They give the answers that keep the funds. We barely have 20 professionals in this country – and in these international organisations, are they real birders in charge? Or statisticians?"

We break for coffee, Steve draws on his e-cigarette, and we're off again.

"So I went to Egypt. I had been in Turkey with a group, birdwatching. I got an SMS from my cousin – from next month the first Hungarian charter of tourists to Egypt are looking for someone who speaks English, Hungarian and Romanian. So I became a guide, it was horrible commerical tourism on the Red Sea coast. In two or three years I spoke Arabic, I saw how the business worked, I quit and began to do it on my own. Guiding, driving, website – birdingegypt. com. And then I was working only with birders.

"I fell in love with the desert and the Bedouin. Wonderful people! I was planning lots of expeditions into the Sinai and a military zone between Sudan and Egypt, the Khalib

Triangle, in the extreme south-east corner. At Jebel Erba and Erkout in Sudan there are mist oases, 20 or 30 kilometres from the sea, where there is a constant humidity. Very few people have seen it. It is magical; I am lucky – I met a safari guy who was related to the Minister of Defence, otherwise no one gets permission. There was one white guy there in 1986 and in 2001 an Italian team.

"The mist oases are like 250 years ago, a plastic bag is a treasure. They make knives out of a piece of acacia for the handle and a blade – they melt the plastic and pour it into the handle as a seal. These are pristine places, one of the last. The wild ass has not been seen since 1933–34. I photographed one there, sent it to a US specialist, she said yes, this was one."

I ask him to tell me about the search for the Slender-billed curlew in northern Egypt.

"The RSPB sent $500 for fuel costs. We went up to the Nile delta, Sinai, Zarniki protectorate. Mary Megdani let us use her house and vehicle, there was a German team and a Czech one. I went to the bird markets alone. All along the Egyptian coast there are bird markets and mist nets, nets for quail and corncrake. There will be 100 kilometres of nets, then a gap, then another 100 kilometres. If you go to Alexandria, El Alamein, to the German Monument, there are nets as far as the eye can see. They can't be removed because the Bedouin, only the Bedouin, have the right to hunt and collect there. My idea was to do a search of the bird markets - along the whole north coast there are 10,000 birds for sale every day. They have passerines, shrikes, raptors . . .

"If I had three or four volunteers, and a day to train them, and they roamed the markets in the migration season, pay a pound or two to the sellers to photograph the birds – you can't act like a conservationist or they will kick you.

We could find it, if it is there. Most of the birds are alive, it's in their interest to keep them alive because they have no way to preserve them."

"That was several years ago. I don't think we had any chance. One million square kilometres, $500, you can't do it. The problem with the bird markets – if a foreigner enters it's a birder. The birds cross the sea so they're really tired, they fly in low on the shore and they're caught."

"Do you think the bird still exists?" I ask.

"If there is still a popluation it exists somewhere in Siberia. They probably don't winter in North Africa – Egypt is really well birded. It probably winters somewhere in Iran. For example the Black Grouse only breeds in one place in Romania. The last observation was in 2007. I went there, spent two days, found the birds. It is really easy to find them if they go there – the challenge is to find them in historical places which are very far and can't be accessed by car. I would go to the Taiga. For three or four weeks, end of May, beginning of June, after that you can't exist because of the mosquitoes.

"If a tiny population migrated through Europe someone would see it, there are so many birders. Almost weekly someone is in Merja Zerga. The last observation in Hungary in 2001 was by Junos Ola. All curlews are shy – at 400 metres they jump up. Usually the Slender-billed curlew mixes with huge flocks of them. He found a flock of 10,000 curlew and said right, today I will find the Slender-billed curlews. He was joking, he spent half a day looking for it and he saw it. It's debated but it looks completely different, it's much lighter – but I have no doubt. If he said he saw it, he saw it."

★

"Why do you do it, Steve – what is the attraction of these data-deficient species?"

He laughs.

"It is some sort of perversion! Everybody focuses on something someone else is doing. It brings money. I am always fascinated by the mystery, by puzzles. I have a whole library of books from the eighteenth century and I am completing a database of Romanian birds. I don't know what I am going to do with it – I have no kids. Maybe someone else! We are already seven billion. This is the thing no one wants to say in conservation – humans. The only hope is Ebola. In Egypt there are 82 million people and the population increases by one million every nine months . . ."

Conservation, Yannis Tsougrakis said, is a game, a mind game: a question of where you choose to look, how you choose to see and what you decide to to do about it. Seen from Steve's perspective the worlds of conservation and ornithology are made of legends as much as truths; they are founded on human tendencies to mythologise, exaggerate and mislead as much as they are built of fact.

"You have heard of the Ivory-billed woodpecker? Someone told me they have found a population in Arkansas. They found it but they don't admit it because all the twitchers in the world will go, to see it, to collect it. He was connected to the National Fish and Wildlife Service. He wouldn't lie.

"And Lord Ilford's woodpecker, there's a story about that. Two were shot in 1989, and it appears in the breeding bird atlas of Romania, only in Dobreaga, in the thick forests, max 100 birds. Each country has to report every six years. I went in March-April. The bird's bill is weak, it needs really old, damaged birch trees. I found the perfect habitat, and all nine species of European woodpecker, but I couldn't find

Lord Ilford's. But it was in Bulgaria, and the Bulgarian and Romanian forests were linked. The record came from this guy Dombrovsky. Then I was in a remote museum in Tulcea and I found an article – a taxidermy catalogue. This guy Dombrovsky was a taxidermist. So he puts it in his catalogue to attract business! When I found this article I knew. So it goes on the Romanian list, and every year copy, paste, copy, paste – no one had gone down there to verify it. This is Europe in the twenty-first century – what do you expect?"

"So what are you working on now?"

"Now I am into the Sand Boa. It's the smallest anaconda, about 60 centimetres long; its northernmost range is southern Bulgaria. It's been seen three times in Romania, 1923 was the last time, but in 2010 someone found a skin. It digs into the sand, it's nocturnal. I was there last week, this place where it could be, arranging with the border guards and the police for two cars plus mine, six to ten persons, to go for a week. Each night we will organise a chain, 10 meters distance between each person – it's a huge area but I am sure we'll find it, under a rock, out hunting."

He pauses and shrugs.

"It doesn't have huge importance but it is in the first category of the European Red List – if we find it, it will be declared protected. This is how we can fight the system – extend the protected zone. If we find it, the guys who can access money will appear but it will be fun looking for it, and if we do expand the protected area they won't be able to build blocks of flats and shopping malls there."

"When species are on such a thin edge one man's intervention can make a difference. To have any goal in your life is to forget about the uselessness of life. To think of interesting ideas . . ."

★

We end up sitting on a bench, me still scribbling, while Steve thinks aloud about the Slender-billed curlew.

"Maybe 30 percent of bird records, historical records, are false. They didn't have very good equipment, it was not exact. Suppose Ushakov didn't find the nest where he said he found it? I would go to the taiga and eat bread for a month and be eaten by mosquitoes if I could see this beautiful bird," Steve declares. "In fact it is impossible there, we would need a helicopter. Then maybe we could flush it – it is quite easy to identify in flight, so no problem."

I think Steve rather optimistic on the last point, but the questions about Valentin Ushakov have been asked for over a century. He is the only man to see Slender-billed curlew nests and publish an account of them. He claimed he found a colony of nests, and his descriptions of encounters with Slender-billed curlews remain a well of mystery and speculation for contemporary ornithologists. Of all the bird-struck men in history, there is probably none who would be half so deluged by questions from today's birders as Mr Ushakov, if only we could ask him.

According to Mr Ushakov

Everything that is known about the nesting sites of the Slender-billed curlew derives from the work of Valentin Ushakov, a native of the Tara region of Siberia, a hunter, ornithologist, writer, naturalist and egg collector.

> With a feeling of deep satisfaction, I watched the magical picture [of 14 Slender-billed curlew nests] and felt very happy, having discovered a new page in the great book of nature. Many fellow ornithologists would give a lot to observe this picture, but I, a humble and ordinary nature-lover, got this chance for free. I warmly thank fate for giving me such inexpressible pleasure and satisfaction. Slowly the sunset was fading, the curlews calmed down; the females sat on nests and the males landed nearby. The calls of the day birds quietened. A bittern started booming more loudly and from above a Jack snipe called melodically. The quiet warm spring night began.*

In 1908, in a large swamp 13 kilometres south-west of Tara, he sees four pairs and shoots one bird, recording that its mate flew around his head uttering pitiful cries. By 1912 the local peasants are telling him the species has declined: at the game market he finds one Slender-billed curlew with 100 Eurasian curlews. In the same year a friend of his sees two and shoots one, and the two men go out searching for them together. They find a pair and a single bird they believed part

---

* Ushakov, writing in 1925, cited in 'Where does the Slender-billed curlew nest, and what future does it have?' by Adam Gretton, Alexander K. Yurlov and Gerard C. Boere in *British Birds* 95, July 2002.

of another breeding pair. In 1914 a hunter brings Ushakov a female and four eggs: Ushakov visited the site and finds a second nest of four eggs, which he collects, and a female bird, which he shoots. In May 1924, outside the hunting season, the laws of which he observes, Ushakov makes his greatest discovery, some 8 kilometres into a 'huge peat bog south of Tara'. He found 14 nests together on an upraised plot on a 'little isle'. Some were little more than a metre apart. All the nests, he wrote, were simple hollows in the ground lined with wisps of dry grass. Clutch sizes varied from one to four.

As he explored the colony the female birds took off in silence, 'approaching me very closely', while the males rushed around his head calling and whistling. Ushakov drew back and watched, and recorded his feelings in the rather wonderful paragraph above.

That is all we have, in summary, but it has been enough to prompt a great deal of effort and attention. The ornithologist Alexander Yurlov has studied the area since the 1980s but has never seen the bird there. International expeditions, each taking two weeks and covering thousands of kilometres, were undertaken in 1989 and 1994. In 1990, thanks to the Soviet Academy of Sciences, a search was made using a helicopter: hundreds of kilometres of otherwise inaccessible taiga were surveyed. In 1997 Alexander Yurlov and Gerard Boere spent five weeks covering 5,000 kilometres and searching likely nesting areas. They found overgrazing, drainage and cultivation had undone several potential nesting sites, but saw other sites that were suitable. The area where Ushakov is thought to have found his colony has changed, with grazing land and forest taking over the marsh.

★

Steve is not convinced by Ushakov: "Once he finds one nest only, then in another year he finds a colony. C'mon, birds are nesting solitary or in a colony, but not both!"

He suspects the best chance of finding one is in its "infinite Asian breeding grounds", and hypothesises that any surviving population might migrate from somewhere in northern central Asia down to wintering grounds in the Persian Gulf, to areas inacessible to western ornitholgists, perhaps in Iran. This would chime with a plausible sighting in Oman this year.

The reasons for the Slender-billed curlew's decline lie in the breeding area, he suspects: drainage and the shrinking of wetlands are obvious factors, but Steve points especially to Adam Gretton's paragraphs in the International Action Plan for the Slender-billed curlew published in 1996: "The level of use of agricultural chemicals in the Aral Sea area (since the 1950s) has caused widespread concern, and has been held responsible for widespread human illness and high levels of child mortality. The lack of water in the area would serve to concentrate such chemicals still further, and could contaminate Slender-billed curlews via their food, or directly in drinking water.

"There are (unconfirmed) reports of nesting Slender-billed curlews from Ust-Kamenogorsk and Semipalatinsk (Gavrin et al. 1962) in the 1920s and 1930s. The main nuclear testing ground of the former U.S.S.R. is just west of Semipalatinsk, and was used until very recently. In earlier years atmospheric tests were conducted here, presumably causing major contamination. Summer records of the species are also known from the Chelyabinsk region (Gavrin et al. 1962), and in recent years very high levels of radioactivity have been found in the environment near Chelyabinsk–40 (E. Nowak verbally). At present we do not have enough information to assess whether such factors could have affected the Slender-billed curlew, but the possibility cannot be entirely ruled out."

Thus exists a possibility beyond irony: that *Homo sapiens* wiped out *Numenius tenuirostris* with a nuclear weapon.

The Hero of the
Danube Delta

Meeting Steve Moldovan is hugely energising and inspiring, but the story of the nesting areas leaves one with a feeling of hopeless unknowing. In a sense this unknowing is the bird's last hope: if it does survive, off the known map of its previous routes and habitats, then so much the better. The discovery of a nest, or even the confirmed sightings of individuals, would have repercussions right through the birding world, particularly at the more militant end: a nest site would need to be kept secret, ornithologists say, and at the same time, somehow, protected.

The next leg of the journey takes me back to Bucharest by train, and to a meeting, the following morning, with Cristian Mihai. Cristian is a stork-like man with a beguilingly mournful face who trained as an aeronautical engineer and now works in publishing. He lives in Bucharest with his wife and two daughters. Initially he is not forthcoming about his life: his passion, an interest which seems to exclude all others, is photographing birds. As he says, "It is something like hunting." Over the three days we spend driving to and around the Razim-Sinoe lake system on Romania's Black Sea coast Cristian spots and names almost every bird we pass. Just watching them, he says, is 'boring'. What he really wants to do is obtain the best possible photograph of species against the best possible backgrounds in the best possible light.

We survey former Slender-billed curlew sites on the fringes of Lake Sinoe and Razim Lake. This is the region of Dobrogea province known as the 'Grind'. It does rather grind the eye: low rolling horizontals of indeterminate colour descend from wind-turbined ridges, through ploughed land the colour of a shoe's sole to enormous tracts of marshes. The Slender-billed curlew sites have a now familiar aspect: mud banks, red salicornia, and wide inaccessible hinterlands of waters and reeds. This is one of the last places the species was recovered in Europe: these are unconfirmed sightings, but a Ukranian ornithologist, Mykhaylo Zhmud, claims four birds seen here in August 2003, six on the 11th of August 2004, and another on the 12th of August 2004. We see several curlews and many other species, but the mission has a funereal feel to it. This is the right place and the right time of year, but the bird is not here, as far as we are able to determine. On the second day we drive north towards the Danube delta and an encounter with a man unlike any I have ever met: Janos Berthond Kiss.

The road north from our base at Sinoe towards Dr Kiss' residence in the hamlet of Iazurile, near the village of Agighol, on the southern edge of the Danube delta, is a delight. It follows the edge of Lake Razim through farmland, the ground rising to the west, where forested slopes descend to pasture. The villages are linked with long, straight roads shaded with poplar trees. Passing through the settlements you are struck by the care and pride the villagers take in their environment. A love of flowers seems universal. Dr Kiss lives in the last house in Iazurile, at the end of a rough track. Even with a satellite map and multiple directions down the phone we are lucky to find it. This is a rich, almost sub-tropical zone, animated with the sway of tall trees and the flights of birds. The migration is well underway: we see flocks of Dalmatian pelicans, a group of red-footed falcons, and many thousands of hirundines, swallows and martins.

Dr Kiss is a Hungarian Romanian from Transylvania. He has white hair, a fine moustache, eyes fiercely clever – he reminds me of Picasso, but kind and modest; he stands comfortably lopsided. He welcomes us with elaborate courtesy and thanks, as if he is invading our home and day. We are given a tour of half the garden, which is large, misleadingly chaotic-looking, and extraordinarily fecund. There are 33 different kinds of fruit trees growing here, and within separate species a dizzying array of varieties and hybrids: he presents a white peach of near-intoxicating sweetness. His press has broken but he is making a variety of different spirits, including calvados and cherry brandy. He offers us raspberry juice.

We prepare for the interview in a covered area beside his house, home to 19 cats, most of them young; some are three-week-old kittens. Dr Kiss says, slyly, that this profusion is his wife's fault – she loves all animals. He clearly does too. Two enormous dogs are banished inside while we talk. As he talks to us – Cristian Mihai acts as interpreter – various cats and kittens climb over him. Sometimes they dig their claws in, but although I see him register the pain he never flinches. His body, which is broad, with the prominent muscles of a farmer or a wrestler, seems of no concern to him. The atmosphere he projects is a strange blend of calm and urgency. He says he finds retirement extremely difficult, hence the garden.

His wife has broken her arm and has gone to see a doctor. She will stay clear of the hospital, Dr Kiss says, because the hospital is a death trap.

Before we start we raise a sip of a dark ruby-coloured spirit, some plum brandy, to the Slender-billed curlew.

"To its memory," says Dr Kiss.

★

"I worked in the wetland for 30 years in the field of conservation and hunting, and in that period the proof of a rare species was to shoot it. In Romanian law all three species of curlew were legitimate prey. It was rare in the sixties and seventies. In those days there was a feeling of security, that things would not change. On a small island close to the coast, Sacalin, there were 15,000 pairs of common terns. Today there are none. If someone had told me this would be possible . . .

"I arrived in 1966 to work at a research station on hunting. This was mostly local hunting, with a small impact on biodiversity, local people hunting for themselves and their families. From the late seventies people began to come from abroad, from France and Italy. Predator and prey evolved together – think of Africa. As men learned to hunt better the animals evolved strategies of escaping them. But when people crossed the Bering Strait into North America they found megafauna which had not evolved these strategies, so humans destroyed the megafauna of North America. The situation in the delta was like this – human population and fauna in tolerable balance.

"Everything changed with the mega-paranoid Communist agriculture: they tried to grab any land of any kind, even what was unsuitable for farming. There was an absolute conviction that wild species were in competition with agriculture. They decided to shoot cormorants, pelicans and egrets. Maybe in England people like nature because it is other to their environment. Here it is not so. The houses of an Englishman amused me because he wanted to be close to nature: small houses, large gardens! And full of flowers, nothing useful like vegetables. And big windows to see out, rather than small ones to protect you!

"The first time I saw a Slender-billed curlew was in a small channel with marshes on both sides. I saw a small pale curlew, like a greenshank pale, and the bill was different. I had my gun and if you ask me today why I did not shoot it I can't tell you. I was a hunter and a biologist, both at once.

"My father-in-law left Romania, together with his sons. He was declared a traitor against the country. My punishment (for being his son-in-law) was to spend three years on an island in the Danube delta. It was a shift of position! I was the prey species! I stopped shooting. I didn't want to, emotionally, and I could see it wasn't a sustainable activity. It wasn't an island like Robinson Crusoe's, there were villagers there. And they started releasing semi-tame mallard ducks for the Italians to hunt. Around 1984–85 the idea was to introduce nandu, a south American ostrich and guinea fowl, and coypu and pheasants, all for hunting.

"I returned to the National Institute for the Danube Delta in 1981. I saw the Slender-billed curlew several times, on the island and on Sacalin island. There is no way hunting caused it to vanish so quickly. It may have been hunted in the Mediterranean, but not here, because it was of no value for food and cartridges cost money. For a period Ceausescu became interested in hunting, so he decided to stop the tourists shooting. I met Ceausescu. He shook my hand. He wasn't even as tall as my dog is long. So hunting stopped for a few years, but now the Italian hunters come again and everyone is complaining about it. They shoot hundreds of larks. Some of them work with people with huge refrigerated lorries.

"We came up with a plan to make the delta a biosphere reserve – me and one other, a piece of paper and a stamp. And I formed a brigade of guards for the delta. Our first employee was a karate master! People were in bad shape, we needed educated people in decent physical condition – where to find them? Karate! We divided the delta into 12 sections, we educated them and prepared them for their jobs. Each person knew his section perfectly. We got a naval officer to teach them where you can hide things on boats, so where they should search. We trained them in vertebrates, mammals, birds and two foreign languages. The first step was guarding, then education, then guiding, then taking groups. It was a beautiful vision and everything was planned and done there, in the delta. There was no Internet connection. It was an organic effort by us, there was no model, and we set it up between 1991 and 1995.

"In 2005 two of my guards caught a high-ranking politician hunting swans in the strictly protected area, which had been a reserve since 1938. This man had been private secretary to the president of the parliament. Calls came to us from the govenor, to my boss. My boss said, 'If I don't fire you they are going to fire me!' I was fired for a few months. Then a new coalition got in, including a Hungarian minority party. They called and said we want you to be Secretary of State in the Environment Ministry. It was a period when things functioned relatively well – they actually put people with knowledge in power!

"My idea was to develop trans-frontier reservations. We succeeded with projects with Bulgaria, to protect rare seals, with Serbia and Hungary. We made a green corridor between Bulgaria, Romania and Hungary, and protected a micro-delta in Ukraine. But no one will remember J.B. Kiss! The other idea was to protect both sides of the Danube where it enters Romania from Serbia at the Iron Gates, to establish environmental management zones on both sides of the border. Nature doesn't respect borders but management authorities do: you have to have the same rules on both sides."

Questions about the possible causes of the Slender-billed curlew's disappearance cause Dr Kiss to grimace and shake his head, the manifestation of a syndrome I now recognise, the frustration of a scientist with insufficient data.

"With the Slender-billed curlew, as a rare species, the impact of hunting on the migration route would be minimal. The wintering areas are so vast it is unlikely minor changes affected them there; for a curlew the spectrum of food sources is pretty large. But Russia today is still effectively a closed country. We don't know what happened there."

"Does it matter if the species is extinct?"

"I think of the ethologist Konrad Lorenz. If someone has a complicated machine and takes it apart, puts it back together, and some parts are not put back in, that doesn't mean they are unnecessary for the machine to work! It is a natural process that everything has a beginning, a climax and an extinction, but if man is involved in producing such a process, in speeding it, it is a great sin. What does the swallow understand of the lake? Nothing.

"If I had shot that bird it would have been in the National Museum's collection, but it would have been a significant part of the population!"

"What is the current situation in the delta?"

"The main problem is fragmentation – what was a large continuous area is now divided into many parts by agriculture. The purple heron needs 20 hectares of undisturbed ground, otherwise it will not breed. There is tourist pressure and extensive fishing. My main concern is construction and the building of tourist developments: it will be a very important negative factor. And there's the boat traffic – boats with large, powerful engines produce waves that disturb birds and destroy nests. You cannot limit the speed – you could limit the engine size."

★

"And the future?"

"We will lose it, the richness of it, and I am happy I am old and I will not see it. The pressure on the protected areas is greater every day, the tension between conservation and exploitation is greater all the time. There are new mining extractions on the Moldavian side, schist, by American companies, and huge pressure at a national level. I started three people in conservation and they are now at the peaks of their careers, but the question is, will they be allowed to do what needs to be done? Most projects in the environmental field are some kind of scam – there is money for meetings, ideas, exchanges, but something real does not necessarily happen."

"But you have trained these people, and the younger generations are acutely environmentally conscious – isn't there hope?"

With a twinkle he returns, "Who says hope is the last thing to die? The Chinese!"

Bursts of Hope
in Bulgaria

We return to Bucharest, discussing families, marriages, birds and people. Cristian's relationship is in difficulties: he is 10 years older than his wife and they married when she was 25. It sounds as though she is longing for a life beyond working at night for a Canadian technology firm, looking after the couple's two daughters and doing the cooking, while Cristian is either at the office or photographing birds. "We will get divorced," Cristian says, "but not yet. My only concern is the girls." As he said it I misheard him and thought, for a second, he said 'birds'.

Bucharest is not a lovely city. Waiting to return the car we watch gangs of young homeless men and women salvaging scrap from a derelict building and carting it off down an alley where they are stockpiling materials they hope to sell. An entirely lost and barefooted young woman with evident mental trauma begs outside a convenience store. Another woman – Cristian diagnoses membership of a 'Protestant cult' by her severe headscarf – buys her soup and bread. The girl looks unsure what to do with it, her face distorted by disappointment that she cannot sell it on. Cristian shakes his head and shows me his photographs from our trip.

The hours we spent sitting in the car beside scummy and polluted plashings overlooked by wrecked factories suddenly make extraordinary sense. Cristian's photographs of little stints, wood sandpipers and, most of all, the sanderlings he stalked across a Black Sea beach, oblivious to the waves and pools and the looks of the last holiday makers, are glowing, beautiful things, transcendent images of birds in a glory which is greater, finer, more luminous than almost anything you could see through binoculars. "Yes," he agrees, "photography is hyper-reality – but look!"

There were occasions, as we edged up to tiny birds in the car, and he called them stupid if they hung around long enough for him to shoot them, and tutted when they flew away, when I was tempted to brain Cristian. I wondered how his wife endured him. Now I realise I have been travelling with an artist. Thanks to Facebook and the birding networks of Bulgaria and beyond, Cristian is not, primarily, a salaryman toiling for a publisher of obscure books, with a small flat in a Bucharest tombstone block, home to two children and an unhappy marriage. Above and before all that, Cristian is one of the foremost bird photographers in Romania, a man with a reputation and a following, a creator, a senior figure to be respected and emulated. He says many younger and less expert birdwatchers contact him with identification questions. I find the pictures bewitching. Who knew a sanderling is so beautiful – a creature made of snow and cream, feathered with light? We embrace in farewell, and Cristian's lanky legs take him down into the metro, tripod over his shoulder. I miss him immediately, though a night without his snores will be a pleasure.

The next leg of my journey is non-stop, overnight to Sofia, then across Bulgaria to Burgas and one of the last Slender-billed curlew sighting spots, the lakes south of the city.

The overnight train from Bucharest to Sofia is a miracle of a machine. It left Moscow at 9.30 yesterday morning, came south to Ukraine, stopped in Kiev, and is now scheduled to depart at 23.50 from Bucharest, arriving in Sofia at 11.02 tomorrow. Massive and magnificent sleeper cars are furnished with plush curtains and a boiler like a giant samovar at the end of each corridor. There is a kind of chef, a huge man like a wrestler, who mostly seems to take care of his own appetite and that of the ticket collector, but who will offer tea with milk or lemon in the morning. I am informed at the ticket desk that no reservations are possible, now. You have to negotiate with the conductor, in euros. The implication of mild bribery is clear. But the trim and manifestly decent man in charge of the sleeping car asks only ten euros over the price suggested by the ticket desk and gives me a compartment to myself: four bunks, a table, and light fittings, catches and trappings all in indestructable chrome. Bedding rolls of clean sheets and mattress covers, blankets and pillow cases are issued. This train could cope comfortably with hundreds of night passengers, but there are only a handful of us. We sway and click out of Bucharest, moving solidly, steadily into the night. For the first time I wish it were a longer journey. Romanian and Bulgarian customs interrupt sleep but briefly with a flash of torches and a perusal of my passport, and unexpected courtesy.

By sunrise we are well into Bulgaria; as the morning lengthens we pass through limestone canyons and Sofia comes too soon. The station looks more destroyed than ever, as if it has suffered an attack of dilapidation or a bombing raid in the last few days. Soon I am on the last train of the journey, the long, slow hauler to the coast. We arrive in Burgas at evening, after many delays. During one pause the dilapidated station where we stop is hymned by choirs of turtle doves, a species so diminished in western Europe that their soft croonings are an almost vanished sound. It is a lovely, soothing echo of an older, richer world. Large floods having reduced the track to a single usable line in several places we take slow time, and arrive after dark. Burgas, it is immediately clear, is an enclave of relative prosperity: a functioning port and a tourist destination, thanks in part to the notorious Sunny Beach resort. The Hotel Bulair is cheap, damp, beloved of mosquitoes and runs a savage breakfast regime – you pay extra for orange juice, sachets of jam and more than one hot drink. Petar Iankov, a luminary of the Bulgarian Society for the Protection of Birds, appears. He is fine featured and white bearded, with an impish aspect and energy. I ask him how his birdwatching life began.

"When I was young all youth groups in Bulgaria were controlled by KOMSOMOL – everything was controlled by the Communist Party. You could not do anything outside KOMSOMOL and it was absolutely formal – meetings, reports, banquets. One year before the changes we applied to create a group, a Society for the Protection of Birds, to be part of the Union of Scientists. We didn't believe it could be granted. We applied in 1987 and waited a year for a response. In March 1988 there was a decision by the Politburo to allow us to create a separate Bulgarian Society for the Protection of Birds – separate! Not part of the Party! Amazing – it was the first thing in the whole scientific area that was not going to be controlled. I think they already knew what was happening in the Soviet Union and they weren't bothered about us; we weren't political, purely conservation. Actually our main attitude was to do something real – not just blah blah! We could see the destruction of forests and wetlands. We started with two simple actions – food for vultures in the Rhodope Mountains and platforms for breeding terns in Lake Atanasovsko.

"There were heavy anti-raptor campaigns in Bulgaria, they thought raptors were pests. In 1984 a terrible thing – the Communist government of Bulgaria made the Turkish population, one million people, change to Bulgarian names. Roads were blocked, villages invaded, their passports were taken, their names were changed. A lot of Turks left. The eastern Rhodope mountains had been heavily populated with their cattle and sheep grazing freely, so there was a lot of food for vultures, but then maybe 400,000 of these people emmigrated to Turkey between 1984 and 1987. Their mosques, their traditional dress were all banned. It was terrible. I had many friends there: if I met them and I used their names – hi Hasan! – someone would report us. This area had been a great example of human-natural cooperation. They had a very tolerant attiude: if a wolf kills a sheep they said 'Allah gives, Allah takes!'"

Petar spent a lot of time in the Rhodope mountains, studying vultures and feeding them. (From a population that shrank to one pair there now descend 77 pairs of griffon vultures.) Next, the whole world changed.

"Before the changes we did not have knowledge, we had anti-knowledge. I was working in a research institute. Our way was not to start with planning, with a goal, a question, to which you could apply a methodology: we didn't know this method! In Communism you collected data, and 'We will see what happens!' This was the way in economics, in policy, everywhere! This was why the system collapsed.

"Then in 1989, we, the BSPB, got access to world conservation organisations. We had had some contact before – an RSPB group came in 1983, in 1994 a guy from Birdlife International. But now we became part of the family of conservtion organisations. The Bulgarian Academy of Sciences didn't even have a strategy for developing the organisation! The BSPB had one first! It was just like a wild place . . ."

★

"I must have been arrested 10, 15 times. I was arrested near a military airport; I was taking pictures of rooks and starlings – I had been sent by a professor to collect data in the area. I was expecting they'd ask me about it, I was waiting all day, and they came in the evening when I was leaving. I was arrested in Sofia cemetery. I was counting singing birds in Sofia for my PhD: cemeteries are perfect, because two plots equal one acre, but I did not realise they had the whole cemetery under constant surveillance. I was arrested by a man I thought was a grave digger. I couldn't find my form to show them, of birds, I said I'd dropped it. The policeman said it was OK, they had followed me from the beginning. Then I realised every grave is unique, with a name and a date, so if you want to leave a message for a spy – this is why they had it under 24-hour surveillance."

Petar was sent to work in a pharmaceutical factory in southern Bulgaria, a feature of the centrally planned economy being the compulsory relocation of labour.

"There was no job for me there, but then someone said a documentary film unit needed someone to find birds' nests to film and I got the job. Then I worked in the zoology department of the Bulgarian Academy of Sciences as an ecologist."

The most extraordinary part of the story of the Bulgarian Society for the Protection of Birds comes after the fall of the Iron Curtain, in the chaotic new world which then emerged.

"We persuaded the government to declare 30 percent of Bulgaria a Specially Protected Area under EU law. 11,000 square kilometres! Because we had the data – we had been collecting data since 1994 and when there came an obligation to declare such areas in 2006 the government didn't have any data – but we did! We had really sound data, not even the Bulgarian Academy of Scientists had it, but we did. We filled in the forms on behalf of the government. BirdLife International had told us how to monitor and collect data, so we did, and the minister just signed it. Bulgaria has 420 species of bird and only 23 can be hunted.

"The EU law is fantastic for Bulgaria. People can apply for money, for cash directly for them, to protect areas where there are corncrakes, for example. The government isn't interested because they can't steal it. Protecting the corncrake, the imperial eagle, the Egyptian vulture – people are getting cash, and we don't need to fight them. They understand! People are actually interested in protecting geese.

"The RSPB taught us how to do it. They said we are not coming to you with a colonial idea, this is your nature, your society, but we find there are two ways to behave as an NGO. You can fight the government, and you will be very popular if you oppose and criticise articles in the newspapers, but our experience shows this is not best for nature. The other way is to work with them. Nine out of 10 times you will fail, but one time what you are fighting for will pass. Mostly you will be disappointed but at any time you will be able to discuss with them. We found some very good people in government who thought like us, people who didn't want money, but wanted to make things better, not many, but a few, and we work with them.

"There are many attempts to corrupt us and intimidate us but we are not five people any more. They cannot kill us or corrupt us by attacking one individual."

We set off for the Slender-billed curlew sites, and Petar talks about the situation of his country.

"Our population has fallen, two million people are abroad. The government is still the same people, the same families as under Communism. These are the same guys but worse and are well educated, they have been to Cambridge or wherever, they are much more dangerous now – they know all these political tricks, how to talk for half an hour without saying anything. But there have been dramatic changes for the better. Some habitats have been destroyed but many more people care. Six years ago we organised the first protest flashmobs in Sofia. They were trying to take the biggest Bulgarian reserve out of the protected area. With social media we got several thousand people to come out. We blocked the streets, the trams, the traffic. There were families, people with children, students – they are always frightened of the young people. We blocked everything for 20 minutes, then the journalists who were listening to the police radio said they are calling in special forces, so we moved. But the atmosphere was amazing. I have never seen anything like this in Bulgaria."

It worked. The reserve, Strandzha National Park, was saved.

We tour the lakes of Chenge Skele and Atanasovsko, the last places in Bulgaria where the Slender-billed curlew was seen. Petar saw one in January 1993 during the winter wildfowl count. The lakes are wide, heavily hedged with reeds, and what mudflat areas there are are reduced, at the time of our visit, by high water levels due to recent rain. At Atanasovsko there is the glasswort which must be associated with the birds' favoured prey species, and much salt panning. At Chenge Skele there are fishermen and large ships at anchor in the middle distance. These are working waterways, but they still possess enough hinterland and marsh, and bird species, to give sancturay to migrating curlew, if such survived. Petar is sure they no longer come here: his teams survey all the Burgas lakes systematically every two weeks. I ask him what lessons he draws from the disappearance of *Numenius tenuirostris*.

★

"It is like a friend is dying and I cannot do anything. On this earth things happen and we cannot do anything, and if we don't know why then sooner or later it will be our turn. This is the most important message – this is beyond our control.

"Second, this is a bird which lived near us. Look – there is the big international road to Turkey, and this is a big harbour, but it was here. We don't really know where it was breeding, what happened or why it declined, we don't know the specific message and we don't know if the reason affects us.

"Third, as a conservationist, I feel a bit responsible for this. The Slender-billed curlew, the Egyptian vulture – I am given consciousness, something they do not have; they are not responsible for me but I am responsible for them.

"If they can go so quickly, in one human life, the people left will have to deal with the consequences. If it is all just cars and apartments, if that is all we care for, then our children and grandchildren will inherit a horrible environment.

"I am much more sensitive now to the danger for the Egyptian vulture because of the Slender-billed curlew. This was the species which showed us how quickly things can change, can worsen."

We leave the lakes and head for the conservation centre at Poda, a dramatic example of the legacy of a life in conservation such as Petar's, and a luminous illustration of the importance of the Burgas wetlands.

All the conservation sites at Burgas can be accessed by roads; indeed, the E87, a major north-south route linking Odessa in Ukraine with western Turkey threads its way between the lakes and wetlands. The conservation centre at Poda sits on a narrow neck between Burgas Bay and the extensive Lake Mandrensko. The neck is a series of parallel roads running through marshes, with all the pylons, channels and works of a suburban post-industry.

The Slender-billed curlew was seen on this isthmus of reed beds and mud banks between 1951 and 1958, and again, infrequently, up to 1975 when an oil refinery was built here. The polychaeta and oligochaeta sea worms which are thought to comprise a part of its diet were in abundance in the area before the refinery turned the marshes into oil spill pools.

"The spoonbill and glossy ibis had gone," Petar says. "In 1989, after the refinery closed and was dismantled in the 1980s, we proposed a Specially Protected Area here. We sited the centre to block the access road because people were using it as a rubbish dump. We built platforms down there for the fishermen so they wouldn't disturb the birds."

The reserve is now a mosaic of pools and marshes between the lake and the road. It enjoys the highest levels of protection under Bulgarian and EU law, covering 100 hectares of reclaimed and restored wetland. The vistors' centre is a three-storey wooden building, popular with Bulgarian and international visitors, and schools. Three buckets of binoculars stand waiting for them. The centre's roofs are flat and railed, perfect birdwatching platforms. As Petar talks a number of visitors with small children appear. The centre's young staff show them where to point their binoculars.

"If you dig down you will come to a layer of oil in the ground," Petar says, "But it does not effect the birds now. We have recorded 273 species here."

He all but glows with enthusiasm and pride. The centre and the reserve are triumphant demonstrations of what can be achieved. Every parent, student and child through the gate is a hope for the future. It is not just a case of identifying birds. Yuri, one of the centre's young staff, obviously proud of his Google t-shirt, is involved in negotiations with power companies over the insulation and marking with reflectors of many hundreds of miles of high-voltage power lines. "They see it is good for them – it costs them money when the birds short the lines: they need our help."

Petar talks about the changes in Bulgaria, and the non-changes, the power and corruption still visited on the country by ruling cliques descended from the Communist Party and backed, to an alarming degree which passes unknown or unmentioned in the West, by Russia.

"We were so blind – I was so blind. I didn't know! They talked about Socialism – what we had here was not Socialism. You see Socialism in Sweden and Denmark! A book came out in the 1980s about Fascism, a very good book. A friend gave it to me before it was banned – it was banned very quickly. But when I read it I thought my God – my God! This is what it is – it is exactly the same as Fascism!

"When we first went to the West, to Austria, to Vienna, my wife burst into tears in front of a sweet shop. She loves sweets – she couldn't believe there were so many! Then at a pedestrain crossing she burst into tears again. We didn't have them in Bulgaria. She couldn't believe these people in these cars were actually stopping and smiling and waving us across. She said this will never happen in Bulgaria! But it does happen now, maybe not the smiles, but we are getting there slowly. We lost 50 years of life in this country. Bulgarians are pragmatic people but the younger generations are sensitive. They're not political, but when they came out onto the streets for that demonstration it was a fantastic atmosphere – I had never seen anything like it."

We stand on the roof and take in the huge views over Burgas, the lakes and the distant hills. We are looking, Petar explains, at the narrowest point of the Via Pontica flyway, the great skyroute for birds migrating between Scandinavia, eastern

Europe and Russia down to the Bosphorus, the Levant and Africa. At Burgas the flyway is only 40 kilometres wide, a great funnel of birds which use the thermals generated by the mingling of land and water below them to gain height for the next leg of their journey. As the morning warms hundreds of white pelicans are working their way upwards in great ragged spirals. They turn and glide, flap and realign, their lines shimmering, seeming to dissolve and reform as they angle throught the thermals, up and up. When they reach a good height they join in skeins, in long V-formations of dozens of birds, and set themselves towards the south.

Lesson from a Ghost

One of the last views of Bulgaria for a traveller flying out of Burgas airport is Lake Atanasovsko, also one of the last places the Slender-billed curlew was seen in Europe. With its boundaries of roads, runways and salt works it seems an unlikely place for a creature of such delicate appearance and mysterious habits – mysterious to us, at least. As the plane pulls up through the warm air, past pelican height and on up through the cloud base, I begin to think that it is not just the disappearance of a bird I have been tracking, but the disappearance of that bird's time, which can equally be measured in human terms.

The Slender-billed curlew first came into the widespread consciousness of European ornithologists through the work of Valentin Ushakov in the 1920s. (Ushakov records that he was taken aback by the volume of correspondence his paper provoked, and by how much time he had to spend answering queries.) This period in Russia was the time of Lenin's New Economic Policy, a limited concession to capitalism and private enterprise which saw Russia's peasant farmers given permission to harvest and sell their own grain, beyond the strictures of collectivisation. The bird began to decline, by Ushakov's account, through this period, but it saw off Lenin and his policies, as it would eventually see off Stalin and his successors, surviving into the era of Gorbachev and Glastnost, and little way beyond that into the present, if the unconfirmed sightings in Ukraine in 2010 were accurate. While the curlew's population dwindled Communism gave way to the post-Communist era in its eastern breeding grounds, while in the West, on its migration route, capitalism and the dream of a united Europe blossomed and flourished. But the bird saw that era end too. The Europe it migrated to in the second half of the twentieth century is gone. The possibility of a united, confident and prosperous continent is fractured and beset by flagging growth, stagnation, unemployment and political paralysis in the face of a resurgent and aggressive Russian expansion. Nationalism, insecurity and hostility to migrants rises everywhere. The Slender-billed curlew, which seems gone from Europe, if not the world, existed alongside optimistic Europe, and leaves behind something which seems less a continent than an archipelago of countries, tossed on the seas of globalisation.

The areas in which it might yet survive, Siberia, Ukraine, Iran and Syria, are currently beyond the reach of British and European birdwatchers. The extensive and intensely admirable efforts to find it and help it, funded by western European conservation organisations and undertaken by volunteers and professionals from over 30 countries, will not be repeated. But though they ended in failure these efforts give hope and pride to this story: it may have come too late, but *Homo sapiens* did try to help *Numenius tenuirostris*.

Perhaps the most invigorating aspect of this tale is the way the bird links a collection of intensely idealistic and effective people across national boundaries. Many are now reaching retirement, or engaged in other projects, and the funding for their works and visions has been drastically cut in recent years. But the story of the Slender-billed curlew is also a story of a great generation of conservationists. Their legacy, in protected areas, reserves, information centres, visitor numbers and inheritors, and the people they recruited and trained to continue their work, has a value which is incalculable. From the beginnings of modern birdwatching and conservation in Greece, Bulgaria, Romania, Italy and other curlew-visited countries of Europe to the present situation, in which great reserves do exist, and invaluable wetlands are protected and visited, the journey I undertook shows, again and again, that passionate efforts by very small numbers of committed people can have a tremendous effect on the planet and its inhabitants, whatever their species.

The true story of the disappearance of the Slender-billed curlew may never be known: the consensus among those best-placed to know is that a combination of habitat loss and degradation of the non-breeding areas and over hunting are likely to be behind its decline, but it is impossible to be certain. The message for us contained in the bird's disappearance has been repeatedly addressed in the preceding pages: again, what it may augur is disputed, but the destruction of wetlands, increasing appropriation of water and land for agriculutral purposes, increased use of pesticides and fertilisers and human pressure on the wetland migration spots are likely to have damaged the species. Its preference for a particular, liminal environment – the strips of tidal saltmarsh which are neither dry land nor submerged for long periods – may well have been part of its undoing. With increasing floods and droughts these areas are more likely to be either dried out or inundated. On my journeys it was routinely the case that water levels were higher than in previous years and saltmarsh areas were reduced. This may have been coincidental but it was strikingly common.

Perhaps this is a message from the Slender-billed curlew: the marshes, the soft overlaps of water and land, are shrinking. Human activity leaves little room for environmental ambivalence. Marshes are often, now, governed into a particular use, either drained or flooded. If the coming hundred years see disputes over water usage in southern Russia, the Balkans, Europe or North Africa it may come to be said, in hindsight, that the quiet, almost invisible fate of the Slender-billed curlew was a sign of troubles to come.

I wish I had seen one or heard one of these beautiful, delicate birds. A world in which only the robust survive is a dulled and blunted planet; all crows, no colour. But if the reaction of those who did see it – the melancholy of George Handrinos, the frustration of Yannis Tsougrakis, the detachment of Janos Kiss and Petar Iankov – is a guide to what it feels like to glimpse one, then perhaps it was better not to have seen it. The report I have recently received from Oman sounds hopeful. Steve Moldovan believes that Ushakov's records are questionable, and that there may be a colony far away from where he said he saw it, which would mean that the subsequent searches in the taiga near Tara in Siberia were concentrating in the wrong place. No one has yet declared the Slender-billed curlew extinct, so it exists out there as a possibility. Instead of lamenting over a world in which fringe-dwellers like this bird are crushed, it is still possible to celebrate a world which is still too large, too diverse and too mysterious for a species such as this to be easily found. Perhaps it will live on for many years in unconfirmed sightings. I hope so. Too much certainty is a miserable thing, while the unknowable has a pristine beauty and a wonder with no end.

Acknowledgements

The Royal Geographical Society (with IBG) made these journeys and this book possible. The Society works in partnership with Neville Shulman CBE – author, explorer and philanthropist – to present the Neville Shulman Challenge Award. For their generosity, faith and much tested patience I would like to thank Mr Shulman, Director of the RGS, Dr Rita Gardner CBE, Grants Officer Juliette Scull (Juliette – thank you a hundred times!) and her predecessors Will Fitzmaurice and Joanne Sharpe; Catherine Souch, Head of Research and Education, and all the staff of the Society who must have considered this the most overdue of projects, and with the most numerous excuses attached to it, and sighed, and allowed me a little more time, and then a little more. Any good that comes from this book is the gift and responsibility of Neville Shulman. Thank you, Sir.

Nicola Crockford coordinated the Birdlife International search on behalf of the RSPB: Nicola, thank you so much, for so much. Tim Cleeves, aka Mr Slender-billed curlew, was sweetly open to my advances. I am fortunate in having the right friends to call when challenged to find the world's rarest bird. Barnaby Rogerson put me in touch with William Blacker, author and scholar, whose deep love and knowledge of Romania will be familiar to readers of his wonderful memoir *Along the Enchanted Way*. William put me in touch with Jean-Marc Mitterer: the kindness and knowledge of these men is wonderful.

In Greece the legendary George Handrinos, Eleni Makrigianni and Yannis Tsougrakis, in Transylvania the extraordinary Steve Istavan Moldovan, in Bucharest my friend, driver, guide and ornithological tutor Cristian Mihai, in Belgium Didier Vangeluwe, in Bulgaria the generous and estimable Peta Iankov, at the BBC Bristol Natural History Unit Tim Dee, Andrew Dawes and Brett Westwood, and in London Rob Ketteridge, Mohit Bakaya, and especially Julian May of the BBC Radio Documentaries Unit are the men and women responsible for the events described in these pages. I would also like to thank Achilles V. Constantakopoulos of Costa Navarino for his company and generous hospitality, and for the ride in his helicopter, which gave a dazzling perspective on the coast of Messinia. Thank you, Peter Browne of Condé Nast Traveller, who commissioned my explorations of the Peloponnese.

My initial searches in Morocco were accompanied by Rebecca Shooter and Robin Tetlow-Shooter, necessitating Robin's absence from school, which was permitted by the Nalin sisters of Aleardo Aleardi, International School of Verona. In Sicily and the Peloponnese I was also accompanied by Rebecca: best and most beautiful of fellow travellers, thank you.

My numerous correspondents and friends, virtual and actual, who gave help, suggestions and tips are too numerous to mention here: thank you.

During the research and writing I was blessed indeed by the love and scholarship of my parents, Sally Clare and John Clare, and the companionship and endless kindness and support of my brother, Alexander Clare (who gave me the keys to his flat). Also in London, Merlin Hughes, Elizabeth Mann, Anna Rose Hughes and James Mann have enabled this and other books partly by keeping the author roofed and off the street. In Cordoba Nicholas Tresillian, in Hay-on-Wye Peter Florence and Maisie Sather, in Penderyn Roger Couhig, in Verona Diarmaid Gallacher and in Rochdale the Shooter family, the golden Jennifer in particular, gave time and kindness I will always fail to quite repay. Thank you. Aubrey Shooter Clare was very forbearing when he wanted to play and I had to work. Thank you, darling Bug.

Little Toller Books, publishers of surpassing good taste and venturesome spirit, made and paid for this book. Thank you Adrian Cooper, Gracie Cooper, Graham Shackleton, Jon Woolcott and Bea Forshall, whose wonderful illustrations adorn the jacket and pages of this book: congratulations all, on your beautiful work.

I would personally like to thank my mentors, superstar Sarah Dunant, Niall Griffiths and Debs Jones, Julia Bell, Laura Barton, Helena Drysdale, Jim Perrin, Jan Morris, Jay Griffiths, Anna Gavalda and Robert Macfarlane, fellow and much greater writers, who show by word and deed how our trade can be practiced, and who define its current heights.

This book is dedicated to the memory of Michael Jacobs, best of men, superlative travel writer, scholar, gentleman and my Hay wingman – or was I his? – whom I hope might have enjoyed this story, and whose spirit informs and infuses my philosophy and approach when on the road. We all miss you, dear Michael, and never meet but we speak of you. May you rest in peace and revelry.

H.C.
Hebdon Bridge, 2015

Published by Little Toller Books in 2015
Lower Dairy, Toller Fratrum, Dorset

Text © Horatio Clare 2015

The right of Horatio Clare to be identified as the author of this work has been asserted by him in accordance with Copyright, Design and Patents Act 1988

Jacket and chapter illustrations © Beatrice Forshall 2015

Typeset in Garamond by Little Toller Books

Printed in TJ International, Cornwall

All papers used by Little Toller Books are natural, recyclable products made from wood grown in sustainable, well-managed forests

A catalogue record for this book is available from the British Library

All rights reserved

ISBN 978-1-908213-33-4

SIGH

SO
AXIO
DELTA

ITALY

GREEC

MOROCCO